Steam Finale
Scotland

Brian J. Dickson

Ian Allan
PUBLISHING

Cover:
Saturday 21 March 1964
Class A1 4-6-2 No 60152 *Holyrood*
prepares to depart from Edinburgh's
Waverley station at the head of a
passenger train to Berwick-upon-
Tweed as ex-LNER Class B1 4-6-0
No 61147 leaves with empty stock
for Craigentinny sidings.

Title page:
Saturday 13 July 1963
Picking up speed with a southbound
express, ex-LMS Class 5MT 4-6-0
No 44786 makes plenty of smoke as
it passes Strawfrank water troughs.

Above:
Saturday 20 June 1964
One of a class of only 10 locomotives,
Standard Class 6P5F 'Clan' 4-6-2
No 72008 *Clan Macleod* makes a
fine sight as it breasts the summit
at Beattock with a six-coach local
passenger train heading for Glasgow.

First published 2003

ISBN 0 7110 2879 6

Published by Ian Allan Publishing
an imprint of Ian Allan Publishing Ltd,
Hersham, Surrey KT12 4RG.
Printed by Ian Allan Printing Ltd,
Hersham, Surrey KT12 4RG.

Code: 0302/B1

This book is dedicated to my wife for her
perseverance and patience.

Contents

Introduction

THIS is one railway enthusiast's photographic and very personal (rather than all-encompassing) record of the final few years of steam locomotive working in Scotland. It covers the period from 1960 to 1966 and cities from Aberdeen to Dundee and Edinburgh to Glasgow. Other areas visited include the Borders and Fife with meanderings to Stirling, Grangemouth, Strawfrank water troughs and the South West area around Dumfries.

In Scotland, 1960 dawned with approximately 50% of the inter-city passenger traffic and the bulk of the goods services still steam-hauled. An Edinburgh enthusiast could still reach Aberdeen, Dundee, Perth, Stirling and Glasgow behind a steam locomotive, and many of the services on the main trunk routes to England were also still the haunt of steam. Steam traction was used on the passenger trains to the West Coast main line from Princes Street station in Edinburgh (until its closure in 1965), and the long-distance services to Carlisle over the Waverley Route from Edinburgh remained virtually 100% steam-hauled. Even the East Coast main line still saw some steam activity on a few passenger trains, the summer-only, non-stop 'Elizabethan' service to/from London being maintained by Haymarket- and King's Cross-allocated Class A4s fitted with corridor tenders. Goods trains were almost exclusively worked by steam power, and the coal traffic around Edinburgh and the Fife coalfields remained almost entirely in the hands of ex-NBR and ex-LNER 0-6-0s, with the heavier and longer-distance coal trains being handled by a variety of larger locomotives, including ex-WD 2-8-0 and 2-10-0 types.

Similarly, in Glasgow and southwest Scotland, a large number of passenger services were still steam-hauled. The majority of goods trains were also still hauled by steam locomotives; the vast amount of coal being moved from the Ayrshire coalfield in the early 1960s was mostly hauled by veteran ex-Caledonian 0-6-0 classes and ex-LMS Class 5 'Crab' 2-6-0s. The four main passenger stations in Glasgow still saw the arrival and departure of most of their services behind a steam locomotive, and it was not until the introduction of the 'Blue Train' electric services operating from both Central and Queen Street stations that the enthusiast saw a major reduction in steam-locomotive allocations at the Glasgow depots.

As the 1960s progressed and more reliable diesel locomotives were delivered, the larger, more powerful steam locomotives were relegated to minor routes and goods trains, whilst the older and less powerful classes went to the scrapyard. Passenger services from Edinburgh to Aberdeen and Dundee became primarily handled by BRCW Type 2 diesel locomotives (working in tandem) or English Electric Type 4s. Services between Edinburgh (Waverley) and Glasgow (Queen Street) had been turned over to Swindon-built DMUs in the late 1950s, and many remaining branch and suburban services were now also being handed over to DMU operation. Likewise, passenger trains on the East Coast main line to/from London were taken over almost completely by English Electric Type 4s or the powerful Type 5 'Deltic' locomotives hauling such important trains as the 'Flying Scotsman', whose timing had been improved to six hours for the 393 miles from Edinburgh. At Glasgow's Central and St Enoch stations, named express-passenger trains such as the 'Caledonian' and the 'Thames–Clyde Express' were being handled respectively by English Electric and BR/Sulzer 'Peak' Type 4 locomotives.

Undoubtedly one of the highlights of steam in Scotland during those final years was the reintroduction, in the summer of 1962, of a three-hour timing for some of the express-passenger trains between Aberdeen and Glasgow (Buchanan Street). In the Scottish Region timetable for the winter of 1964/5 there were seven trains advertised in each direction, of which the two most important morning and evening departures each way were scheduled to travel the 153 miles in three hours, stopping only at Stonehaven, Forfar, Perth and Stirling. These were not particularly difficult timings for the lightly loaded trains of seven or so coaches, but the trains still had to cover the long, sweeping almost 90 miles of fast-running line between Aberdeen and Perth in 96 minutes, with two intermediate stops. Drafted in to operate these trains between 1962 and 1966 were some of the remaining ex-LNER Class A4s, which were allocated to Aberdeen Ferryhill and Glasgow St Rollox depots. Until the summer of 1966, when these services

were finally 'dieselised', the 'A4s' had a virtual monopoly. Locomotives transferred during this period included Nos 60004 *William Whitelaw*, 60007 *Sir Nigel Gresley*, 60009 *Union of South Africa*, 60016 *Silver King*, 60019 *Bittern*, 60024 *Kingfisher*, 60026 *Miles Beevor*, 60027 *Merlin*, 60031 *Golden Plover* and 60034 *Lord Faringdon*, and throughout these four years they were kept immaculately clean by both the responsible depots. Running over the ex-Caledonian main line via Forfar to Perth, these trains were both a joy to travel on, and to watch from the lineside. No wonder they became a magnet, drawing enthusiasts from all over the country to enjoy this last great flourish of main line steam in Scotland. Unfortunately all good things must come to an end, and, as the summer of 1966 came to a close, the five Aberdeen-based survivors that were operating the service — Nos 60004/9/19/24/34 — were withdrawn.

During the years 1962-6, Perth station became a huge draw for steam enthusiasts, as it saw not only the Aberdeen–Glasgow expresses but also a mass of traffic heading to/from the West Coast main line with fish, parcels and postal trains, in addition to the normal passenger

Sunday 29 March 1964
Ex-LMS Class 8P 'Coronation' 4-6-2 No 46256 *Sir William A. Stanier, F.R.S.* being turned on the turntable at St Margarets depot in Edinburgh (see pages 86-89).

traffic — the vast majority of it still steam-hauled behind a variety of locomotive types. These ranged from ex-LMS, ex-LNER and Standard 4-6-0s to ex-LMS, ex-LNER and Standard Pacifics, with a thin sprinkling of pre-Grouping 0-6-0s still used on local goods trains and shunting duties.

Another of the highlights, resulting from the opening in 1963 of the two large marshalling yards at Kingmoor in Carlisle and Millerhill in Edinburgh, was the increased amount of goods traffic which traversed the Waverley Route until its closure in January 1969. The difficult and sparsely populated terrain covered on this route may have deterred its use for large numbers of passenger trains, but this was certainly not the case for goods trains where this alternative route into Scotland's capital and the central belt was heavily utilised. During the early 1960s the bulk of this traffic remained steam-hauled. An enthusiast did not have to travel far out of Edinburgh to witness the procession of heavy goods trains heading in both directions. On a warm summer's day, Stow and Heriot stations could be comfortable spots to watch this traffic working hard on the down trains approaching Falahill Summit, hauled by some of the most powerful locomotives still working on British Railways. St Margarets depot in Edinburgh and Canal — and, following that depot's closure in the summer of 1963, Kingmoor — in Carlisle supplied examples of all four ex-LNER Pacific classes, along with 'B1s' and 'V2s'. Ex-LMS classes were also in evidence, with 'Black Fives' making regular appearances and 'Royal Scots' and even 'Jubilees' occasionally being seen.

During the early 1960s the Five Nations rugby tournaments still generated huge amounts of special passenger traffic, with trains bringing supporters to the matches at Murrayfield in Edinburgh. The highlight was undoubtedly the biennial match against Wales held in the Scottish capital. The influx of Welsh supporters would usually start with a trickle on the Thursday before the Saturday match, building with a greater number arriving on the Friday and finally swelling to enormous proportions with the arrival of up to a dozen or so trains on the Saturday morning. The majority of these special workings would arrive at Princes Street station, but there would be some arrivals at Waverley that had taken the slightly shorter but more difficult Waverley Route from Carlisle. In the early 1960s all of these trains were still steam-hauled and would bring motive power not normally seen by enthusiasts in Edinburgh, including a number of 'Jubilees' and 'Royal Scots' from Crewe and occasionally Liverpool and Manchester. In alternate years the traffic would be in the reverse direction, with special trains leaving (not just from Edinburgh) to make the long haul to Cardiff. In February 1964 I made the trip to Cardiff, the first leg to Carlisle being handled by Class A1 4-6-2 No 60152 *Holyrood*, and I well remember witnessing its struggle to climb to Whitrope Summit, on a wet night, from a standing start at Hawick station with a load of 13 coaches.

The early 1960s were also exceptional for the activity of special branch-line tours, with trains visiting goods-only or soon-to-be-closed branches. One of the most widely travelled was that of the SLS/RCTS in the summer of 1960, which spent a week visiting lines from the Black Isle (north of Inverness) to Aberdeenshire, Fife, Tayside and Perthshire, using a variety of pre-Grouping locomotive types that were fast disappearing. These included ex-CR 4-4-0s and 0-6-0s and ex-NBR 0-6-0s. A highlight of this tour was the use of the preserved locomotives which the Scottish Region had recently returned to traffic — HR 'Jones Goods' 4-6-0 No 103, GNSR 4-4-0 No 49 *Gordon Highlander* and NBR 4-4-0 No 256 *Glen Douglas*. Other, more local one-day tours included the 'Pentlands & Tinto' in 1961 using ex-CR Class 2P 0-4-4 tank No 55124, which traversed the old Caledonian line to Broughton. Others in 1962, 1963 and 1965 visited such diverse places as Methil, Leslie and Crail in Fife, Macduff, Turriff and Old Meldrum in Aberdeenshire, Jedburgh and Duns in the Borders and Govan, Renfrew, Greenock and Lanark in the West. Several other day tours visited the branches around Edinburgh and East Lothian.

The early 1960s saw the rapid withdrawal of the remaining pre-Grouping types of locomotive, with many depots having long lines of ex-NBR and ex-CR tank and tender locomotives awaiting removal to the scrapyard; a visit to Bo'ness dock, where rows of ex-Caledonian locomotives were stored, would confirm this. By the mid-1960s the more modern steam locomotives also started to become redundant, and the storage lines at depots became filled with ex-LNER Pacifics, 'B1s' and 'V2s'. Class V1 and V3 2-6-2 tanks, meanwhile, disappeared almost overnight from Edinburgh when the suburban service was turned over to DMUs; Bathgate depot, near Edinburgh, stored a number of these locomotives before they went for scrap. Kittybrewster depot in Aberdeen likewise played host to a large number of locomotives made redundant by the 'dieselisation' of all traffic to the North; several ex-LMS Class 2P 4-4-0s were stored here, along with the four ex-GNSR Class Z4 and Z5 0-4-2 tanks that had for many years worked the lines in Aberdeen harbour.

Compared with their English counterparts, the Scottish pre-Grouping companies have fared badly in terms of locomotives surviving in preservation. The tally amounts to only 10 locomotives — three Caledonian, three North British,

two Highland (one of these being in a Canadian museum) and one each from the Great North of Scotland and Glasgow & South Western companies. We have the London, Midland & Scottish Railway to thank for saving two of these and the early management of British Railways' Scottish Region for another two. Of the other five, four are down to quick-thinking societies or individuals and one to the Glasgow Transport Museum. The Highland could have had another representative, but the failure of British Railways to take decisive action saw No 54398 *Ben Alder*, which had been in storage for many years, cut up for scrap in 1966.

Today there are several shining beacons that rose following the departure of main-line steam in 1968. Through the forward thinking of individuals and societies, acquiring

Saturday 25 August 1962
Duddingston & Craigmillar station on the Edinburgh suburban line, shortly before its closure to passenger traffic. All the ephemera of the period is here — the lattice ironwork footbridge with its warning notice, the ornate lamp and the telegraph pole with wires. Passing through is Standard Class 4 2-6-0 No 76105, built at Doncaster in 1957, with an eastbound goods train.

locomotives, coaches, wagons and old or disused railway lines and working hard over many years at restoration, Scotland now has four lines that give the modern enthusiast, the general public and the tourist a view of the infrastructure and motive power that was once regularly seen in use on British Railways' Scottish Region.

Aberdeen

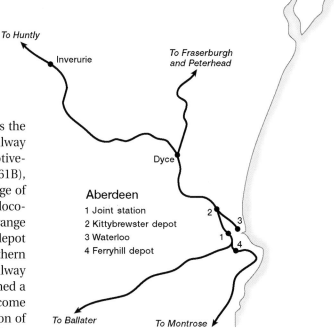

I always looked forward to holidays in Aberdeen, as the city contained many areas of interest for the railway enthusiast. During the early 1960s the two motive-power depots were visited regularly, with Ferryhill (61B), the ex-Caledonian Railway depot on the southern edge of the city, bustling with movements; as it supplied the locomotives for all the services to the south, it stabled a range of ex-LMS, ex-LNER and Standard locomotives. The depot was finally closed to steam early in 1967. On the northern side of the city, the ex-Great North of Scotland Railway (GNSR) semi-roundhouse at Kittybrewster (61A) seemed a quieter depot. Closed to steam in mid-1961, it had become a servicing depot for diesels, following the introduction of these locomotives on all the traffic north of Aberdeen. Nevertheless, it still had rows of steam locomotives stored out of use and awaiting their fate. One unusual sight to be witnessed in the morning was the turning of the overnight TPO mail coaches from England on the depot's turntable.

The present Joint station, opened in 1915, was itself always busy with arrivals and departures, to the north the diesel traffic to Inverness and the coast branches, but to the south the majority of traffic was still steam-hauled, with the highlights of the day being the arrival and departure of the three-hour services to Glasgow, usually behind an ex-LNER Class A4. Other services to Perth and the south were still steam-hauled, and most goods traffic still arrived and departed behind a steam locomotive, ex-LMS 'Black Fives' and ex-LNER 'V2s' being the most common. Guild Street goods yard, adjacent to the station, was still despatching a couple of fast fish trains southwards each day, usually hauled by a Class A2 or similar Pacific.

By 1960 passenger traffic on the Ballater (or 'Royal Deeside') line was handled primarily by the unique two-car battery-operated multiple-unit, plus the occasional steam working using a Standard '4MT' 2-6-4 tank. The line was closed in 1966, although there are currently (2002) plans to reopen a short section at the Ballater end. Surprisingly the battery-operated multiple-unit survived into preservation and will hopefully one day be seen again working on the Deeside line.

Early morning in Aberdeen harbour witnessed a scene of hectic activity, with huge numbers of fishing boats disgorging their catches for the market, but calm would descend mid-morning; then coal vessels could be seen unloading into wagons that were destined for the gasworks just off Regents Quay. The gasworks had a small fleet of steam locomotives, with two working examples. One of these would often be seen trundling to Waterloo goods yard to pick up oil tank wagons. Waterloo yard was the site of the original Aberdeen terminus of the GNSR, opened in 1856, and in the early 1960s the remains of the old station were still standing, with a couple of veteran ex-GNSR coaches parked under the overall roof.

Inverurie Works was opened by the GNSR in 1902, leading to the closure of Kittybrewster Works in Aberdeen. It was sited just over 16 miles north of Aberdeen and was easy enough to reach by train for a half-day visit. In the early 1960s it still undertook some repairs and overhauling of steam locomotives and was beginning to handle the servicing of the diesel locomotives then being introduced. It also carried out large-scale carriage and wagon repairs and was finally closed at the end of 1969 with the loss of many valuable jobs to the local economy.

From Aberdeen it was possible to make a day trip to Tillynaught, where the old GNSR branch to Banff struck off from the main line, and this remained the last steam-hauled passenger working north of Aberdeen, following 'dieselisation' of all other services. On the day I visited I was the only passenger to be seen.

Tuesday 27 August 1963
At Tillynaught, Standard Class 2 2-6-0
No 78054, built at Darlington Works
in 1955, prepares to run round its
train before heading off to Banff. This
branch of the erstwhile GNSR
remained steam-worked until closure
in July 1964.

Saturday 18 May 1963
Ex-LMS Class 5MT 4-6-0 No 44931
reverses out of Ferryhill depot,
making its way to the Joint station.
In externally good condition, it was
allocated to Perth (63A) depot and
would probably be working a
passenger train to Glasgow.

Saturday 18 April 1964
Heading for Kittybrewster goods yard
in the north of the city, Class 5MT
4-6-0 No 44721 drifts under the large
signal gantry protecting Aberdeen
Joint station approach.

Saturday 18 April 1964
Riddles-designed ex-War Department
Class 8F 2-8-0 No 90705 backs slowly
towards the coaling plant at Ferryhill
depot.

Saturday 17 October 1964
Aberdeen Gasworks was reached by rail from Waterloo goods yard along the cobbled Waterloo and Regent quays in the harbour. Here Aberdeen Gasworks 0-4-0ST No 3 proceeds along the quay to pick up oil wagons at Waterloo yard. This beautiful little locomotive, built in 1927 by Andrew Barclay (No 1889), has survived and is currently to be seen at the Grampian Transport Museum at Alford, where it is preserved as a static exhibit.

Saturday 18 April 1964
Having worked into the city earlier in the day with a freight train (see page 10), Class 5MT 4-6-0 No 44721 makes a splendid sight heading south past Ferryhill depot with a passenger train.

Saturday 18 April 1964
Inverurie Works was just over 16 miles from Aberdeen and at this time was still servicing steam locomotives. The smokebox/boiler/firebox combination, possibly from a 'Black Five', appears to be surplus to requirements.

Saturday 18 April 1964
The remains of veteran Reid-designed ex-NBR Class J88 0-6-0T No 68332 were still being used to supply power at Inverurie Works.

Monday 26 April 1965
Ex-LMS Class 5MT 4-6-0 No 44998
sits at the head of a train of empty
coaching stock in Aberdeen Joint
station. The locomotive is in gleaming
ex-works condition and is spending
a few days running-in after overhaul
at Inverurie Works. Its final destination
would be its home depot of Perth
(63A).

Dundee

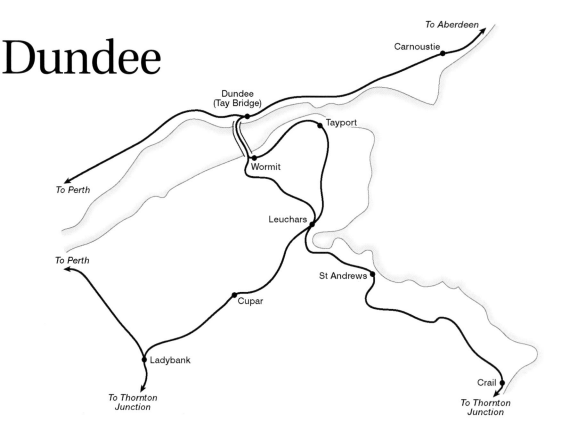

FAMOUS for its rail bridge, jute manufacturing, children's comics and two good football teams, Dundee was still a fair-sized railway centre in the early 1960s, with Tay Bridge depot (62B) needing an allocation of larger locomotives such as ex-LMS and Standard Class 5MT 4-6-0s and Standard Class 4MT 2-6-4 tanks. It was also still busy enough to need some smaller 0-6-0 tender locomotives to service the few remaining local freight-only branch lines in the area. It was briefly noteworthy for its allocation of two LNER-designed Class A2 Pacifics, Nos 60528 *Tudor Minstrel* and 60532 *Blue Peter*, which were used on both goods and passenger traffic to Aberdeen, Perth and Glasgow.

The rail bridge itself and the journey over it would always bring sombre thoughts of the dreadful events of the night of Sunday 28 December 1879. The original single-track bridge designed by Thomas Bouch was almost two miles long and opened on 1 June 1878. Due probably to design and building faults, the high girder section collapsed during a tremendous storm, sending the locomotive and its train of six coaches, with 75 passengers and crew, plunging into the stormy waters of the River Tay. There were no survivors. The bridge was rebuilt to a design by W. H. Barlow with double track and reopened on 20 June 1887. The story of the disaster was immortalised in the awkward rhymes of the poem penned by the eccentric Dundee resident poet, William Topaz McGonagall.

By 1963 the line from Dundee to Leuchars Junction via Newport-on-Tay East and West stations, on the southern side of the River Tay, had been truncated to Tayport, and the branch trains from Dundee were being hauled by Standard Class 4MT 2-6-4 tanks. Two years later the service was being handled by a two-car DMU.

My last visit to Dundee in July 1965 turned out in hindsight to be a unique and lucky day for an enthusiast. Having arrived at Edinburgh Waverley expecting the train to Dundee and Aberdeen to be hauled by the usual pair of BRCW-built Type 2 diesels, I was extremely pleased to see a gleaming ex-LNER Class A4 backing onto the carriages. This turned out to be No 60007 *Sir Nigel Gresley*. On arrival at Dundee Tay Bridge station, I took the branch train to Tayport, and this journey allowed me to photograph Class A2 No 60532 *Blue Peter* leaving Tay Bridge goods yard at the head of a goods train for Aberdeen. Both these splendid locomotives survived into the safe hands of preservationists and for many years have brought enjoyment to the public by working special trains throughout Britain.

On an overcast day in 1960, an
unidentified ex-LNER Class V2 2-6-2
heads out across the Tay Bridge with
a train from Aberdeen to Edinburgh.
The truncated piers of the ill-fated
first Tay rail bridge can clearly be
seen alongside the later structure.

Saturday 17 July 1965
On this wonderfully sunny day,
Class A2 4-6-2 No 60532 *Blue Peter*
heads north from Tay Bridge goods
yard with a goods train for Aberdeen.

Saturday 17 July 1965
Allocated to St Rollox depot (65B),
this Standard Class 5MT 4-6-0
No 73152 was one of 30 of the class
introduced in 1956 fitted with Caprotti
valve gear. This locomotive was built
at Derby in 1957 and was one of a
batch of 10 allocated to the Scottish
Region of British Railways.

Saturday 17 July 1965
The midday summer sun casts sharp shadows at Tay Bridge depot as veteran ex-NBR Class J36 0-6-0 No 65319, bearing a Tay Bridge (62B) shed code, simmers after a morning's duty in the area. The row of telegraph poles stretching into the distance are a magnificent reminder of the period.

Saturday 17 July 1965
The second of the pair of Class A2s allocated to Dundee Tay Bridge depot, No 60528 *Tudor Minstrel* simmers outside the shed.

Fife

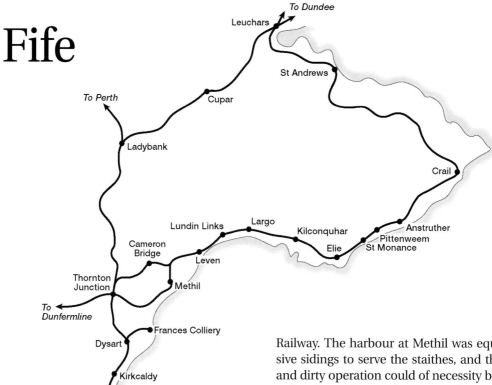

THINKING about railways in Fife during the early 1960s still conjures up memories of two very different types of lines. Firstly, those serving the huge coalfield of central Fife, stretching from Methil in the east to Cowdenbeath in the west with Thornton Junction almost at its centre. The deep-shaft collieries across the area and their adjoining railway yards were many, with both British Railways and the National Coal Board providing hard-working locomotives to move large amounts of coal to the cities, towns, ports and power stations on the northern side of the River Forth. Railways for carrying coal only were extensive around Methil and the Fife coast southwards to Kirkcaldy, where the National Coal Board had extensive facilities for the repair and maintenance of locomotives. Visiting some of the collieries in the area, such as the Frances and the Wellsley, an enthusiast could see many examples of Andrew Barclay-built 0-4-0 and 0-6-0 tanks at work. At Methil the ochre-liveried locomotives of the Wemyss Private Railway brought trains of coal from the collieries in the Wemyss area for off-loading into boats at the coal staithes in Methil harbour. Fortunately one of these large Andrew Barclay-built 0-6-0 tank locomotives has survived and is to be seen at the Bo'ness & Kinneil

Railway. The harbour at Methil was equipped with extensive sidings to serve the staithes, and this extremely noisy and dirty operation could of necessity be working 24 hours a day, depending on how many boats were waiting to be loaded. At Kirkcaldy itself, next to the passenger station, was sited one of the famous linoleum works which prompted the well-known lines from the poem 'The Boy in the Train' by Mary Campbell Smith —

> *For I ken mysel' by the queer like smell,*
> *That the next stop's Kirkcaddy*

— and to this day the odour is still often to be noticed as the train pulls to a stop.

The alternative was to view the beautiful farming countryside through which the railway ran from Thornton Junction to the fishing villages of the 'East Neuk of Fife'. These villages, such as Elie, St Monance, Pittenweem, Anstruther and Crail, all supported small fleets of fishing vessels which could be seen unloading their cargo on most weekday mornings. Passenger traffic on the 'East Neuk' line was light, except for holiday periods, when seaside villages such as Leven, Lundin Links and Largo would become busy with day-trippers from Edinburgh and Glasgow.

By the mid-1960s the passenger service on the 'East Neuk' line was down to four diesel multiple-unit trains each way per day to/from Edinburgh or Glasgow and one steam-hauled stopping train from Crail to Thornton Junction. The freight traffic had been reduced to one steam-hauled, pick-up goods train per day.

Saturday 15 September 1962
Ex-LNER Class J38 0-6-0 No 65901 pounds westbound past Thornton Junction depot with a train of loaded coal wagons. In the background is the now closed and demolished Rothes Colliery.

Saturday 15 September 1962
Ex-LNER Class J38 0-6-0 No 65902
is also heading west past Thornton
Junction depot with a mixed freight.
This very powerful class of
locomotive, classified '6F' by British
Railways, was a Gresley design
introduced in 1926 specifically for
these types of traffic in Scotland.

Monday 14 October 1963
Working a pick-up freight servicing
the stations between Inverkeithing
and Thornton Junction, ex-NBR
Class J37 0-6-0 No 64586 shunts the
small yard at Dysart station before
moving on to the Frances Colliery
to collect loaded coal wagons.

Tuesday 15 October 1963
Kirkcaldy station had a busy goods yard serving the surrounding factories, including the famous linoleum works, and the small harbour in the town. This was a typical scene at this time, with steam and diesel traction working side by side. Hunslet-built 0-6-0DM No D2583 shunts in the yard whilst ex-LNER Class J38 0-6-0 No 65901 waits to move off with a stopping freight train to Thornton Junction.

Tuesday 15 October 1963
Ex-NBR Class J37 0-6-0 No 64550 hurries past Kirkcaldy station with a ballast train heading north to Thornton Junction.

Saturday 19 September 1964
The driver's view from the footplate of ex-LNER Class B1 4-6-0 No 61103, approaching Anstruther station on the afternoon passenger train from Crail to Thornton Junction on the 'East Neuk' line.

Saturday 14 September 1963
National Coal Board 0-6-0ST No 7
of the East Fife Area is working
in the yard at the Wellsley Colliery,
near Methil. The fireman is preparing
to couple the locomotive to some
wagons.

Monday 14 October 1963
Having shunted the yard at Dysart
station and descended the gradient
to the Frances Colliery (at the edge
of the River Forth) with empty coal
wagons, ex-NBR Class J37 0-6-0
No 64586 prepares to lift a train of
full coal wagons from the yard back
up the hill to Dysart.

Monday 21 September 1964
Having worked into Crail during
the morning, the driver of ex-LNER
Class B1 4-6-0 No 61103 prepares to
make an inspection of his locomotive
before leaving Crail with the
afternoon passenger train to
Thornton Junction.

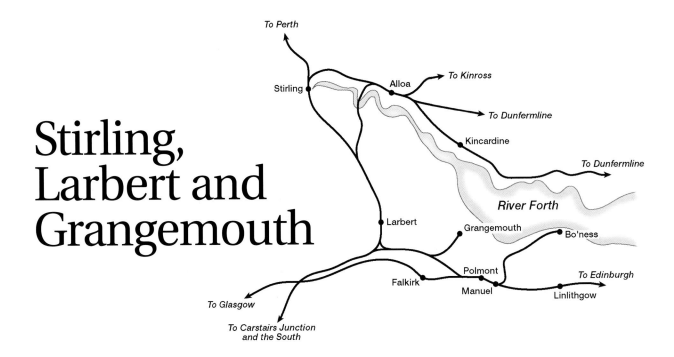

To Perth

Stirling

Alloa

To Kinross

To Dunfermline

Kincardine

To Dunfermline

River Forth

Larbert

Grangemouth

Bo'ness

Polmont

To Edinburgh

Falkirk

Manuel

Linlithgow

To Glasgow

To Carstairs Junction
and the South

Stirling, Larbert and Grangemouth

I N the early 1960s a railway enthusiast could still spend a very exciting day visiting Stirling and Larbert stations and then travelling on to Grangemouth to visit the depot and docks there. Lying on the main line between Glasgow and Perth, Stirling still had a very busy railway scene, with local traffic to/from Alloa, Dunfermline, Edinburgh, Glasgow and Perth and a large number of through trains between Glasgow and Aberdeen, Inverness, Perth and Oban.

The present station was completed by the Caledonian Railway in 1915/16 and is probably still one of the most attractive in Scotland, with its crow-stepped gables, a fine concourse with ornate ironwork supporting a large glazed roof and a wide sweeping staircase linking the main station buildings by a footbridge to the remaining platforms.

The level of traffic through Stirling could produce a wide variety of locomotive types, with ex-LMS and Standard Pacifics on passenger, parcels and postal workings and, of course, ex-LNER Pacifics working on the fast three-hour passenger trains between Glasgow and Aberdeen. Goods traffic could bring ex-LNER Class B1s or V2s, along with ex-LMS and Standard Class 5MTs. Local passenger workings to Edinburgh and Perth were in the hands of Standard Class 4MT 2-6-4 tanks.

Stirling motive-power depot, by then renumbered 65J, still had a small allocation of ex-CR 0-6-0 tender locomotives used for local branch freight workings, but as these closed the locomotives were sent for scrap, and the depot finally closed in December 1966.

Larbert lay at the junction of the main line from Glasgow to Perth with those to Edinburgh, Grangemouth and the main line to Carstairs Junction and the South. Situated about eight miles south of Stirling, it saw very similar through traffic. Trains from here additionally served Grangemouth, and these were still steam-hauled by ex-LMS or Standard Class 5MT 4-6-0s.

Grangemouth station was a simple affair with one very long platform, but the adjoining yards and depot serving the docks were extensive. Vessels from all over the world unloaded their cargoes here, but traffic to/from the Far East was particularly evident, with the famous 'Ben Line' boats using Grangemouth as their Scottish home. During the early 1960s the motive-power depot (65F) still housed a wide variety of locomotive types ranging from ex-CR and ex-NBR 0-6-0s to ex-LMS Class 5MT 4-6-0s. It also housed a number of the powerful Riddles-designed ex-War Department 2-8-0s and 2-10-0s for the heavy freight trains out of the docks. The depot was closed to steam in 1965, but the building survived almost intact until demolition in 2000.

Sunday 29 February 1964
One of the hardest-working classes
of locomotive used for all types of
traffic in Scotland was the Standard
Class 4MT 2-6-4 tank, whose
reliability, sure-footedness and pace
of acceleration were well known.
Here we see No 80060 making a very
lively start away from Stirling station
at the head of a train of empty
coaching stock.

Left:
Saturday 26 January 1963
Ex-LMS Class 5MT 4-6-0 No 45461, equipped with a small snowplough, waits to leave Grangemouth station on a Glasgow-bound passenger train. The locomotive was allocated to Perth (63A) depot.

Above:
Sunday 29 February 1964
Standard Class 5MT 4-6-0 No 73148 coasts towards Stirling station at the head of a passenger train bound for Glasgow. This locomotive, built at Derby in 1957, was one of only 30 of its class fitted with Caprotti valve gear, 10 of which were allocated to the Scottish Region.

Below:
Sunday 29 February 1964
Standard Class 7P6F 'Britannia' 4-6-2 No 70036 *Boadicea* waits to leave Stirling station with a passenger train for Aberdeen. She appears to be in need of some vital maintenance, judging by the amount of escaping steam.

Saturday 17 July 1965
Ex-LMS Class 5MT 4-6-0 No 45084
waits to leave Stirling station at the
head of a passenger train to Perth.
The shed code (65J) indicates that
the locomotive is allocated to the
depot at Stirling.

Sunday 6 July 1963
Ex-LMS Class 5MT 4-6-0 No 45357
enters Larbert station with a
passenger train heading
for Glasgow.

Sunday 29 February 1964
Class 5MT 4-6-0 No 44724 heads
north out of Stirling station with a
passenger train for Perth. Note on the
cabside of this locomotive the tablet-
exchange equipment, which was
used on the extensive single-line
sections of track in the North and
West of Scotland.

Edinburgh

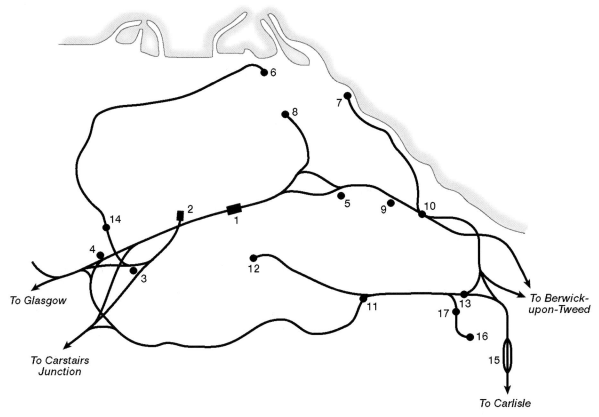

To Glasgow

To Carstairs
Junction

To Berwick-
upon-Tweed

To Carlisle

1 Waverley station
2 Princes Street station
3 Dalry Road depot
4 Haymarket depot
5 St Margarets depot
6 Leith North station
7 Seafield depot
8 Leith Central station
9 Craigentinny carriage sidings
10 Portobello
11 Duddingston & Craigmillar station
12 St Leonard's goods depot
13 Niddrie West Junction
14 Murrayfield station
15 Millerhill marshalling yard
16 Woolmet Colliery
17 Niddrie Brick Works

Edinburgh:
Princes Street Station

THE Caledonian Railway arrived in Edinburgh with a line from Carstairs Junction in 1848 and built a temporary terminus at Lothian Road. It was not until 1894 that the splendid and cavernous red-stone terminus, fronted by the famous hotel facing into Princes Street, was opened, with the hotel itself being opened in 1903.

Branches radiated from the terminus to Balerno, Barnton, Granton, Davidson's Mains and Leith North, with passenger services surviving to the latter until April 1962. Goods traffic serving the paper mills on the Balerno branch lasted until late in 1967. Most of the trackbed on these branches has since been turned into cycleways or footpaths. There was also connection to and extensive sidings serving Leith docks and its very busy trade, particularly with the countries and ports around the Baltic Sea. A junction made from Dalry Road to Haymarket West on the North British line heading west from Waverley station gave the Caledonian access to Larbert, Stirling and the North.

Trains from Princes Street served the South via the West Coast main line at Carstairs Junction, and British Railways' Scottish Region winter timetable of 1964/5 shows nine trains leaving for Carstairs Junction each weekday, with through carriages to Carlisle, Manchester (Victoria), Liverpool (Exchange), Crewe, Birmingham (New Street) and London (Euston).

Passenger traffic between Edinburgh and Glasgow had not always been the sole property of the North British Railway and its shorter route from Waverley station. The Caledonian line from Princes Street via Shotts may have been a few miles longer and may have served a less populated area, but the 1964/5 timetable shows that 10 stopping trains were still running in each direction on weekdays. Furthermore, in the Shotts area it served a number of collieries, which produced a large amount of coal traffic for the line.

For an Edinburgh enthusiast, Princes Street station, known locally as 'the Caley', was almost unique in that all passenger traffic, right up to its closure in September 1965, was steam-hauled. Following the opening of the Duff Street connection between Slateford and Haymarket in 1964, the station was closed on Sundays, traffic arriving and departing from Waverley station, but during weekdays the sounds and smells of steam continued.

Today the railway terminus may have been demolished and the former trackbed to Dalry Road turned into the Western Approach Road, but the famous hotel facing into Princes Street still proclaims the name 'Caledonian', as a reminder of the railway that built it.

Sunday 2 July 1961
Ex-LMS Class 4MT 2-6-4T No 42204
leaves the station in charge of a train
of empty coaching stock heading
for the carriage sidings.
This locomotive was one of the
Fairburn developments of a Stanier
design; the shed code (66E) shows
that it was allocated to Carstairs
Junction depot.

Sunday 2 July 1961
Having just arrived at the head
of a passenger train from Carstairs
Junction, Standard Class 5MT 4-6-0
No 73059 sits within the cavernous
interior of the station.

Saturday 5 October 1963
Ex-LMS Class 5MT 4-6-0 No 44799 leaves the station with (according to the headcode) an ordinary passenger train — probably a stopping service to Carstairs Junction.

Monday 25 March 1963
Ex-LMS Class 5MT 4-6-0 No 45361 prepares to leave the station with a train for Glasgow Central via the Shotts line. At this time, when all the Edinburgh Waverley–Glasgow Queen Street trains were served by diesel multiple-units, the Edinburgh Princes Street–Glasgow Central services were still steam-hauled and would remain so until Princes Street's closure in September 1965.

Saturday 5 October 1963
Local enthusiasts watch the
departure of a passenger train to
Carstairs Junction behind ex-LMS
Class 5MT 4-6-0 No 44953.
This photograph gives a hint of
the cavernous interior of the station
and also shows the signals protecting
the exits from the platforms.

Saturday 5 October 1963
Under very cloudy, rain-laden skies,
Standard Class 5MT 4-6-0 No 73057
approaches the station platforms
with a train from Carstairs Junction.
This locomotive was built at Derby
in 1954.

Saturday 5 October 1963
The rain-clouds have deposited their
cargo and moved on, as ex-LMS
Class 8P 'Coronation' 4-6-2 No 46251
City of Nottingham arrives at the
head of an RCTS special.

Tuesday 14 July 1964
Ex-LMS Class 8P 'Coronation' 4-6-2
No 46255 *City of Hereford* drifts into
the station. The headcode (just
one lamp on the buffer-beam)
is misleading, as the locomotive
has arrived with a passenger train
from Glasgow.

Saturday 11 April 1964
The driver and fireman of ex-LMS
Class 5MT 4-6-0 No 45469 (right)
watch for the imminent departure
of another of the class, No 44702
(left), at the head of a Saturday
football special to Kings Park
station in Glasgow. Again, the
cavernous interior of the station
is very apparent.

Edinburgh:
Waverley Station

WAVERLEY station in its present form was completed in 1897 by the North British Railway, but there had been a station on the site since 1846, when the North British opened a terminus for trains from Berwick-upon-Tweed and the South. The Edinburgh & Glasgow Railway had originally terminated at Haymarket, on the western edge of the city; this railway company was taken over by the North British in 1865, but it was not until 1897 that the tunnels from Haymarket to Waverley were quadrupled and the present station was finally completed. The imposing structure of the North British Hotel was opened in 1902 with, of course, direct links by lifts and staircase to the station concourse below.

Essentially the station was built as a huge island area with 19 platforms and two additional suburban platforms. The East Coast expresses used the through Platforms 1/19 and 10/11, whilst all other passenger traffic used the 15 bay platforms. Waverley provided services to many of the area's branch lines, including those to Corstorphine, Haddington, Leith (Central), Musselburgh, North Berwick, Peebles, Penicuik and Polton; by 1960, however, all but the Corstorphine, Musselburgh and North Berwick branches had lost their passenger services. The local suburban trains, known locally as the 'Sub', operated from Platforms 20 and 21 on an Inner and Outer Circle basis serving the southern edge of the city, but this service was withdrawn in 1962. Until 1960 the 'Sub' service was steam-hauled, latterly using ex-LNER Class V1 and V3 2-6-2 tanks based at St Margarets, but from 1960 until closure it was operated with DMUs. The service to Corstorphine ceased at the end of 1967, leaving North Berwick as the only branch line still served from Waverley. The fine station building at Leith (Central), opened in 1903, gained a new lease of life in the 1960s, when it became the DMU-servicing depot for the Edinburgh area, but this too was closed — in 1972 — and later demolished, a supermarket subsequently being built on the site.

By 1960 most of the named passenger expresses to/from London were diesel-hauled. The prestige 'Flying Scotsman' was turned over to the powerful 'Deltic' locomotives carrying a new winged-thistle headboard, but a few classic sights remained for the enthusiast: the summer-only 'Elizabethan' still ran behind an 'A4', and there were still steam-hauled trains to Aberdeen and over the Waverley Route to Carlisle, occasionally hauled by an ex-LNER Pacific. The early 1960s still saw many regular steam workings into the station, with all the empty-coaching-stock workings from Craigentinny yard usually being handled by an ex-LNER Class B1 4-6-0 banked by a Standard Class 4MT 2-6-4T — and a fine sight they made, finishing their charge up the 1-in-78 gradient into the station.

By 1991 the electrification of the East Coast main line had reached Waverley, and today the station has only 14 operating platforms; some have been filled-in for car-parking use, and several are unnumbered and are for non-passenger use. Controversial plans to redevelop the whole station area also exist and are the subject of discussion between train-operating companies, Network Rail and the local authorities.

Thursday 23 May 1963
The permanent-way gang take a few
minutes' rest as ex-LNER Class V2
2-6-2 No 60855 completes the stiff
climb up the 1-in-78 gradient into
the eastern end of the station
at the head of a passenger train.
It is proceeding over the crossing
that will take it into Platform 10 or 11.

Monday 3 June 1963
In less-than-pristine condition, ex-LNER Class A4 4-6-2 No 60002 *Sir Murrough Wilson,* built at Doncaster in 1938, drifts into the western end of the station at the head of some empty coaching stock. The imposing structure of the Scottish National Gallery sits on the Mound above the tunnels that give access to the station from the west.

Monday 3 June 1963
Sitting in the headshunt at the eastern end of the station, the fireman of ex-LNER Class A3 4-6-2 No 60082 *Neil Gow* trims the coal in the tender before the locomotive reverses onto its train. Note the German-style smoke-deflectors, which were fitted to a number of this class.

Friday 1 February 1963
At the head of a rugby special from South Wales, ex-LMS Class 7P 'Royal Scot' 4-6-0 No 46157 *The Royal Artilleryman* completed its journey to Edinburgh in very difficult conditions. The crew struggled in falling snow with a very heavy train, taking fully 15 minutes to move it from the Calton Hill tunnel exit to rest in the 'Sub' platform, slipping most of the way. Following a brief respite to let the passengers alight, the locomotive is seen leaving the western end of the station with the empty coaching stock.

Saturday 6 July 1963
Railway enthusiasts doing what railway enthusiasts do — watching locomotives at work. In this case the object of their attention is Class B1 4-6-0 No 61324, a St Margarets locomotive, leaving the suburban platforms at the head of a westbound passenger train.

Saturday 15 June 1963
Standard Class 6P5F 'Clan' 4-6-2
No 72005 *Clan Macgregor* reverses
onto the coaching stock for a train
bound for Dundee and Aberdeen.
The 'Clans' were rare visitors to
Edinburgh, especially the Waverley
station. In the background can clearly
be seen the portals to the Mound
tunnels that allow access to the west.

Tuesday 4 February 1964
The wonderful structure of the North
British Hotel stands iceberg-like, over-
looking the station. Known locally as
the 'NB', it was closed for complete
refurbishment in the early 1990s and
reopened as The Balmoral. Local taxi-
drivers, when asked by strangers for
'The Balmoral', pleaded ignorance,
and eventually the owners revised
the name to The New Balmoral,
so the continuity with the old 'NB'
still existed. Ex-LNER Class V2 2-6-2
No 60813 leaves the west end of
the station light-engine, heading for
St Margarets depot. This locomotive
was uniquely fitted with a short
stovepipe chimney and deflector.

Above:
Tuesday 3 March 1964
Standing at Platform 11, ex-LMS
Class 5MT 4-6-0 No 44975 of Dalry
Road depot waits to leave westbound
at the head of a passenger train.
The tracks leading from Platforms 20
and 21 — the 'Sub' — can be seen
on the right.

Top right:
Thursday 5 March 1964
Class A1 4-6-2 No 60129
Guy Mannering leaves the suburban
platforms, heading west with a train
of coaching stock. This locomotive
was one of the class to be named
after characters from the 'Waverley'
novels written by Sir Walter Scott.

Lower right:
Friday 13 March 1964
Class A1 4-6-2 No 60116
Hal o' the Wynd, in a very leaky state,
leaves the suburban platforms with
a train of empty coaching stock.
This locomotive was similarly named
after a character from one of Scott's
novels, *The Fair Maid of Perth*.

Previous page:
Saturday 21 March 1964
Class A1 4-6-2 No 60152 *Holyrood*
was regularly to be seen working
both goods and passenger trains
over the Waverley Route to Carlisle,
but here we see the locomotive
preparing to depart from Platform 9
at the head of a passenger train for
Berwick-upon-Tweed. On the left,
ex-LNER Class B1 4-6-0 No 61147 fills
the station with a mix of smoke and
steam as it leaves Platform 10 with
a train of empty coaching stock
for Craigentinny sidings.

Above:
Saturday 21 March 1964
Making a spirited departure from
the 'Sub' platforms, Class B1 4-6-0
No 61349 of St Margarets depot
heads west with a passenger train.

Right:
Saturday 9 May 1964
Ex-LNER Class A4 4-6-2 No 60009
Union of South Africa emerges from
the eastern end of the Calton
tunnels, at the head of a special train
consisting of Pullman coaches.
The locomotive was bought privately
in 1966 and went on to haul many
special trains throughout Britain.

Saturday 30 May 1964
Ex-LMS Class 6P5F 'Jubilee' 4-6-0
No 45696 *Arethusa* reverses out of
Platform 9, having arrived earlier with
a passenger train from Carlisle.

Saturday 30 May 1964
Having worked its train into Waverley
from the South, Class A1 4-6-2
No 60140 *Balmoral* bursts from the
Mound Tunnel, heading west with
the empty coaching stock.

Friday 14 August 1964
A regular sight at the eastern end
of Waverley was the procession of
empty-stock workings that moved
in and out of the station throughout
the day. Here, Standard Class 4MT
2-6-4T No 80026 arrives with four
coaches. The fireman appears to be
absorbed in ensuring that an injector
has started properly.

Friday 14 August 1964
Another empty-stock arrival,
this time behind Class B1 4-6-0
No 61350.

Monday 13 July 1964
Heading west from the gloom of the 'Sub' platforms, ex-LNER Class V2 2-6-2 No 60955 vigorously lifts its passenger train out of the station.

Friday 4 September 1964
Pounding through the station at the head of a ballast train, the driver of Class B1 4-6-0 No 61308 keeps a sharp lookout as he passes beneath the imposing bulk of St Andrew's House on Calton Hill.

Friday 4 September 1964
Having suffered a fire on board and subsequently failed, BRCW Type 2 No D5305 completes its journey from Hawick behind ex-LNER Class J38 0-6-0 No 65914, which had been sent to the rescue.

Saturday 27 March 1965
Under the impressive clock tower of
the North British Hotel, a busy scene
at the western end of the station.
Class B1 4-6-0 No 61324 moves away
light-engine whilst English Electric
Type 4 No D362 waits to move onto
its train.

Saturday 8 October 1966
Ex-LMS Class 5MT 4-6-0 No 45492,
allocated to Carstairs Junction (66E)
depot (although the buffer beam
has 'Motherwell' painted on it), waits
to leave Platform 10 with empty
coaching stock. Two inquisitive young
enthusiasts discuss some mechanical
detail of the locomotive.

Saturday 30 July 1966
Princes Street Gardens in high
summer, before the 'wires' went up
and when steam still had a few last
duties. Here we see ex-LNER Class V2
2-6-2 No 60919 heading west
out of Waverley station with
a passenger train.

Edinburgh:
St Margarets MPD (64A)

ST MARGARETS was by far the largest depot in Edinburgh, with a history going back to the mid-1840s. The site was both locomotive works and running shed for the North British Railway and straddled the East Coast main line approximately 1¼ miles east of Waverley station. The old works was on the up side, with the main operating shed on the down side. By the early 1960s the old works was used to stable veteran ex-NBR tank locomotives around its small turntable, with a small machine shop supplying and repairing fittings for locomotives.

The main running shed was a long six-road affair with extensive lines for storage and dedicated ashpits. The depot was laid out for access from the down main line, with locomotives moving straight in to be coaled up. These extensive coaling facilities stretched almost the full length of the site and were hand-worked, with coal being shovelled from wagons to tubs ready for tipping into locomotive tenders and bunkers. It was dimly lit, and the site resembled an underground coal working.

The large turntable was sited directly beyond the coaling plant, locomotives being turned as required before moving over the ashpits to have fires dropped and ashpans emptied. Watering followed, before locomotives moved into the shed for inspection.

In the early 1960s St Margarets still had a wide variety of locomotives on shed. Along with the usual Class B1s and V2s there were a number of ex-NBR 0-6-0 classes — 'J35s', 'J36s' and 'J37s' — used on local goods traffic. With most of the collieries in the Lothians area still in operation, these classes, along with a few ex-LNER Class J38s, worked most of the coal trains. Prior to the 'dieselisation' of the suburban passenger trains, St Margarets supplied the motive power in the form of ex-LNER Class V1 and V3 2-6-2 tanks. The depot also provided locomotives for a large number of goods trains working over the Waverley Route and by the mid-1960s was regularly supplying Class A1s, A3s, B1s and V2s for this work. Towards the end of its working life the depot stabled fewer steam locomotives, a number being former Dalry Road examples of LMS origin, such as Class 4MT 2-6-4 tanks and Class 5MT 4-6-0s.

The depot finally closed in April 1967 and was subsequently demolished. Today there is no evidence that it ever existed, the site of the old works on the up side being a car park and the down side containing two large Scottish Office government buildings.

Monday 24 May 1965
Vintage ex-NBR Class J36 0-6-0
No 65234 fulfilling its last duties,
albeit stationary, as a supplier of
power to St Margarets machine shop.
This part of the depot was the site
of the original North British Railway
workshops on the up side of the
East Coast main line.

Monday 15 July 1963
With the main running shed being on the down side of the East Coast main line, there was always traffic to watch proceeding in both directions. Here we see ex-NBR Class J37 0-6-0 No 64624 hustling past the depot at the head of a goods train for Niddrie Yard on the southeastern edge of the city.

Saturday 27 March 1965
Standing under rows of full coal tubs, Standard Class 4 2-6-0 No 76050 waits to be coaled up before moving to the turntable. Built at Doncaster in 1956, this locomotive was withdrawn in September of 1965 after only nine years of service.

Tuesday 2 June 1964
Ex-LNER Class A4 4-6-2 No 60004
William Whitelaw simmers quietly
outside the shed. Built at Doncaster
in 1937 as No 4462, this locomotive
was originally named *Great Snipe*;
it was later renamed after the first
Chairman of the LNER at the time
of the Grouping and would survive
until July 1966. With the closure of
Haymarket depot to steam in 1963,
St Margarets became busier with
the remaining steam locomotives.
The grimy atmosphere shown here
continued until April 1967, when
the depot was closed.

Sunday 19 July 1964
With little Sunday traffic, St Margarets would find itself packed with off-duty locomotives. This particular day saw ex-LNER Class A4 4-6-2 No 60010 *Dominion of Canada* simmering amongst other locomotives on shed. To the right are Class B1 4-6-0 No 61294 and Standard Class 5MT 4-6-0 No 73151, the latter fitted with Caprotti valve gear. On the left are two English Electric Type 4 diesel locomotives, one at the head of the depot's breakdown train. *Dominion of Canada* was withdrawn in May 1965 and is now preserved in Canada.

Saturday 28 September 1963
The depot had an air of constant bustle with locomotives moving straight from the coaling plant to the turntable for turning if required. Class A1 4-6-2 No 60151 *Midlothian* has been turned and is waiting to move into the shed.

Sunday 7 October 1962
The turntable at the depot could accommodate the largest Pacific locomotives. Here, however, we see it turning ex-LMS Class 5MT 4-6-0 No 45175.

Sunday 4 October 1964

The East Coast main line was closed on this day to allow the replacement of the decking on the bridge over Restalrig Road South, next to the depot, all rail traffic being diverted via the Abbeyhill and Piershill loop. Two cranes were used to do the work — a 50-ton breakdown crane, No RS1054/50, together with another, No RS1069. These two photographs show the work proceeding and the new deckings being readied for swinging into place. Several steam cranes of this period have survived into preservation and still work at various railways throughout the UK.

Saturday 27 March 1965
Standard Class 4MT 2-6-4T No 80054 stands on one of the storage roads behind the depot. As can be seen, the fabric of the building was starting to suffer from neglect, with a large number of roof panels missing.

Sunday 4 April 1965
In charge of a special passenger train working south, ex-LNER Class A4 4-6-2 No 60031 *Golden Plover* passes St Margarets depot. In the background, Clayton Type 1 diesel No D8576 stands on the up-side storage line.

Sunday 18 July 1965
Ex-LNER Class V2 2-6-2 No 60970 waits to be coaled up as the driver and fireman, having finished their duty, head for the reporting office.

Saturday 27 March 1965
Class B1 4-6-0 No 61404 receives attention over the ashpits at the back of the depot.

Saturday 27 March 1965
Having been coaled and watered,
ex-LNER Class V2 2-6-2 No 60816
sits quietly over an inspection pit
at the shed.

Top right:
Sunday 4 April 1965
Class B1 4-6-0 No 61397 stands
quietly over an inspection pit
at its home depot.

Lower right:
Monday 24 May 1965
A clutch of Class B1 4-6-0s at the
depot, from left to right Nos 61076,
61191 and 61324.

Sunday 4 April 1965
The grimy atmosphere is evident
as ex-LNER Class V2 2-6-2 No 60846
moves slowly forward through the
depot yard.

Top left:
Sunday 30 May 1965
Ex-LNER Class A4 4-6-2 No 60027
Merlin is in light steam and is being
towed from the back of the yard by
English Electric Type 4 No D263.
The cabside of *Merlin* bears the
distinctive yellow diagonal stripe
indicating that the locomotive
must not work over lines fitted
with overhead electric wires.
Within four months it would be
withdrawn from service.

Lower left:
Sunday 19 July 1964
Ex-LMS Class 6P5F 'Jubilee' 4-6-0
No 45635 *Tobago* pauses on the
up main line, waiting to move over
to the down line and into the depot.
Even at this time, diesel locomotives
were to be seen within this strong-
hold of steam: in the background,
English Electric Type 4 No D305 waits
for its next duty whilst a classmate
stands at the head of the depot's
breakdown train.

Above:
Monday 16 May 1966
By this time, St Margarets had many
fewer steam locomotives to handle,
and a number of those were ex-LMS
types. Sitting quietly in the shed is
ex-LMS Class 4MT 2-6-4T No 42273.

Left:
Monday 16 May 1966
Standing over an inspection pit, ex-LMS Class 4MT 2-6-4T No 42274 of Carstairs Junction depot simmers whilst awaiting attention.
In the background ex-LNER Class V2 2-6-2 No 60868 stands over one of the ashpits.

Top:
Friday 15 July 1966
Towards the end of its useful life, the depot was storing some steam locomotives, and on this day Class B1 4-6-0 No 61345 and an unidentified ex-LMS Class 5MT 4-6-0 stand towards the rear of the shed as the strong summer sun strikes through the deteriorating roof.

Above:
Monday 16 May 1966
Ex-LMS Class 5MT 4-6-0 No 45053 in a very shabby state, with loose cladding bands round the boiler; the locomotive is being prepared for duty, with a crew member oiling the motion. Compare this photograph with that of the same locomotive on page 106, taken over two years earlier.

Sir William A. Stanier, F.R.S.

THE LMS Class 8P 'Coronation' Pacifics were first introduced in 1937, but the last two locomotives in the class — Nos 46256 and 46257 — were in fact H. G. Ivatt developments introduced 10 years later in 1947; both were fitted with roller bearings and had other minor detail alterations. No 46256 was named in honour of William Arthur Stanier, who was responsible for the original design. Born in 1876, from 1892 he had been apprenticed to the GWR works at Swindon, moving to the LMS in 1932 and holding the post of Chief Mechanical Engineer from 1932 to 1944. Knighted in 1943, he died in 1965.

Allocated to Crewe North (5A) depot, No 46256 had been constructed at Crewe works in 1947 and named in a ceremony at Euston station only a few days before nationalisation of the railways. It was withdrawn from service in the autumn of 1964 after working the 'Scottish Lowlander' on 26 September. The locomotive had given only 17 years' service.

Sunday 29 March 1964
Ex-LMS Class 8P 'Coronation' 4-6-2
No 46256 *Sir William A. Stanier, F.R.S.*
is being squeezed onto the turntable
at St Margarets after coaling-up.
The locomotive had worked into
Edinburgh at the head of a train from
Glasgow. The fire would be dropped,
the ashpan and smokebox emptied
and the tender filled with water
before returning to Glasgow.

29 March 1964
Possibly because I was the only enthusiast to witness No 46256's arrival, I was invited onto the footplate to watch some of the operations taking place.

The young fireman in charge of such a prestigious locomotive was probably then about my own age (18), but he was very knowledgeable and answered all my questions whilst managing the disposal, including checking the mechanical lubricators.

29 March 1964
This stranger to Edinburgh, No 46256
is the subject of conversation by some
of the St Margarets staff discussing
the relative merits of this class
against their usual LNER-designed
Pacifics. On the other hand, they may
just be admiring the sheer bulk of
the locomotive.

Prince Palatine

No 60052 *Prince Palatine* was one of the class of 'A3' Pacifics designed by Nigel (later Sir Nigel) Gresley. Constructed at Doncaster Works in 1924, it was originally numbered 2551 and was one of a number of this class named after famous racehorses; its namesake had been very successful before World War 1, winning the Imperial Stakes in 1910, the St Leger and Gordon Stakes in 1911, the Jockey Club Stakes, Doncaster Cup, Eclipse Stakes and Ascot Gold Cup in 1912 and the Coronation Cup and Ascot Gold Cup again in 1913.

   No 60052 *Prince Palatine* became the penultimate working example of the class, the last being No 60103 *Flying Scotsman,* sold into preservation in 1963. For the last few years of its working life No 60052 was based at St Margarets and was to be seen regularly performing over the Waverley Route, hauling heavy freight trains between Carlisle Kingmoor and Edinburgh Millerhill yards. It was withdrawn from service in January 1966.

Saturday 29 May 1965
In beautifully clean condition,
Prince Palatine awaits departure
from St Margarets depot to join
its train at Waverley station.

Monday 16 May 1966
Behind St Margarets depot the remains of two ex-LNER Class A3 Pacifics have been stripped of fittings and are awaiting towing away for scrap. No 60041 *Salmon Trout* and No 60052 *Prince Palatine* (nearer the camera) are in a very sad state; compare this photograph with those on pages 122 and 91, 92 showing the respective locomotives a year earlier.

Saturday 29 May 1965
Heading its special train southwards, *Prince Palatine* picks up speed as it passes Craigentinny carriage sidings. The solitary permanent-way gang member checking fishplates keeps his eyes on his work, missing the splendid sight behind him.

Edinburgh:
Haymarket MPD (64B)

HAYMARKET, on the western side of the city, was Edinburgh's 'Top Link' depot, supplying motive power and crews for the express passenger trains from Waverley station to the South via the East Coast main line. There had been a depot on the site since the late 1880s, and this had been rebuilt and enlarged on several occasions. By 1960 it was established as a large eight-road shed with modern coaling tower facilities, and its allocation of locomotives included examples of all four LNER Pacific designs, with a handful of 'V2s' and 'B1s' and some veteran ex-NBR tank locomotives for local shunting duties.

With the introduction of the 'Deltics' on the named expresses to London and English Electric Type 4s and BRCW Type 2s on the route to Dundee and Aberdeen, Haymarket became the main stabling and servicing point for these locomotives. By late 1963 the depot was closed to steam locomotives, its allocation either going for scrap or being transferred to St Margarets (64A).

An enthusiast visiting Haymarket on a Sunday could usually count on seeing at least one of the depot's long-standing allocation of ex-LNER Pacifics — 'A4s' No 60004 *William Whitelaw* and No 60009 *Union of South Africa* and 'A3' No 60041 *Salmon Trout*. *William Whitelaw* and *Salmon Trout* were scrapped in 1966, but more fortunately *Union of South Africa* was bought privately in 1966 and passed into preservation.

Sunday 31 March 1963
Ex-LNER Class A3 4-6-2 No 60091 *Captain Cuttle*, in externally very poor condition, prepares to leave the depot. The shed code (52B) indicates that the locomotive is allocated to Heaton depot.

Sunday 11 November 1962
Two ex-LNER Class A3 4-6-2s at rest in the depot. On the left, fitted with German-style smoke-deflectors, is No 60088 *Book Law* and on the right No 60053 *Sansovino*. Both are in poor external condition.

Sunday 17 February 1963
On this bright winter's day, with the remains of a snowfall on the ground, ex-LNER Class A4 4-6-2 No 60012 *Commonwealth of Australia* lies out of steam at the western end of the depot, shunted between another, unidentified classmate and an unidentified Class B1 4-6-0. The immense bulk of the depot's coaling tower can be seen in the background.

Sunday 3 March 1963
On this very overcast day, Class A1 4-6-2 No 60160 *Auld Reekie* stands out of steam at its home depot. This was an appropriate allocation, as the city of Edinburgh is nicknamed 'Auld Reekie', due to the large amounts of smoke that used to pour from its chimneys. None of this class passed into preservation, but the A1 Steam Locomotive Trust is currently building (at Darlington) the 51st example of the class, to be numbered 60163 and named *Tornado*.

Thursday 13 June 1963
Designed by Matthew Holmes and introduced by the NBR in 1888, the 'J36' class 0-6-0s had very graceful lines. No 65288, one of several examples working around Edinburgh at the time, simmers at the depot. This locomotive and classmate No 65243 *Maude* were to become the last working steam locomotives north of the border. Fortunately *Maude* has been preserved and can be seen at the Bo'ness & Kinneil Railway near Edinburgh.

Edinburgh:
Dalry Road MPD (64C)

WHEN the Caledonian Railway reached Edinburgh in the late 1840s a depot was opened at Dalry Road. This was sited on the western side of Edinburgh, opposite Dalry Road station, within the junction of the lines from Princes Street station to Carstairs Junction and Leith North. It was very much a traditional Caledonian-style shed, comprising four roads and some storage lines with coaling facilities that were small and basic. Surprisingly the depot had no turntable, relying instead on the 60ft example at Princes Street station; unfortunately this could not handle Pacific locomotives, which had therefore to be turned on the Slateford–Coltbridge–Dalry triangle.

The depot's allocation of locomotives in the late 1950s and early 1960s included ex-Caledonian Railway 0-4-4 tank and 0-6-0 tender locomotives used on passenger and freight services on the branches to Leith North, Colinton and Balerno. Numerous ex-LMS Class 4MT 2-6-4 tanks and Class 5MT 4-6-0s were also allocated here for working passenger turns to Carstairs, Carlisle, Glasgow and Stirling, but what made the depot of more interest to the local enthusiast was the variety of locomotives that could arrive on trains from Birmingham or Carlisle, or even on fill-in turns from Glasgow Central. These ranged from 'Jubilee' and 'Royal Scot' 4-6-0s to 'Coronation', 'Britannia' and 'Clan' Pacifics.

After the opening of the Duff Street connection in 1964, all Sunday traffic for the Caledonian line ran to/from Waverley station. Consequently Dalry Road depot was closed on Sundays other than for the lighting-up of locomotives required for Monday morning (which started late on the Sunday afternoon). With the final closure of Princes Street station in September 1965, the depot itself was closed in October of the same year, being later demolished. Today there is no sign that it ever existed, roads having been built over the site.

Dalry Road was much smaller than either Haymarket or St Margarets, and I am sure that consequently it had a much friendlier atmosphere, with the depot staff and traincrews being much more inclined to take the time to talk to enthusiasts about their locomotives and duties.

Sunday 11 November 1962
Dalry Road depot would be packed with locomotives on most Sundays awaiting weekday duties. Here ex-LMS Class 4MT 2-6-4 tank No 42273 stands beside ex-LMS Class 5MT 4-6-0 No 44975. The tank locomotive, a Fairburn development of a Stanier design introduced in 1945, gained some notoriety in January 1958 when, at the head of a passenger train, it failed to stop in Princes Street station, ran through the buffers and came to rest with its front half resting on the station concourse.

Sunday 17 February 1963
Every few years there would be heavy snowfalls in the central belt of Scotland, and the line between Princes Street and Carstairs Junction, with its open sections at Cobbinshaw, was particularly susceptible to deep-drifting snow. On this day ex-LMS Class 5MT 4-6-0 No 45155, along with classmate No 45367, had been operating a snow-clearing special and on completion of the work had returned to Dalry Road depot for servicing. It is seen here at the entrance to the shed, complete with plough and some remains of its foe.

Sunday 3 March 1963
Ex-LMS Class 8F 2-8-0 No 48756, in poor external condition, stands amid the grimy surroundings of Dalry Road depot. The '8Fs' were very rare visitors to Edinburgh around this time; the locomotive's headcode lamps indicate that it has worked a freight or ballast train into the city, while its shedplate (12A) denotes allocation to Carlisle Kingmoor.

Sunday 7 July 1963
Visiting from Carstairs depot
(66E), ex-LMS Class 5MT
4-6-0 No 45245, in externally
very clean condition, stands
over an inspection pit.

Sunday 20 July 1963
Designed by H. G. Ivatt and
introduced in 1946, ex-LMS Class 2
2-6-0 No 46482 stands on the storage
line. This basic design of locomotive
was perpetuated in the British
Railways era with the introduction
of the Standard Class 2 2-6-0s built
at Darlington from 1952 to 1956.

Saturday 5 October 1963
Having worked an RCTS special into
Princes Street station, ex-LMS Class 8P
'Coronation' 4-6-2 No 46251 *City of
Nottingham* has been turned on the
Slateford–Coltbridge–Dalry triangle
and coaled at the depot's coaling
stage, from where it is seen making
a slippery getaway.

Wednesday 25 December 1963
Christmas Day surprisingly sees
ex-NBR Class J36 0-6-0 No 65243
Maude in steam at Dalry Road depot.
Built in 1891, this locomotive served
with the British forces during World
War 1 and was named after its return
to Britain at the end of the war.
Fortunately it was saved for
preservation and today can be seen
showing off its graceful design at
the Scottish Railway Preservation
Society's line at Bo'ness, near Falkirk.

Thursday 2 February 1964
Ex-LMS Class 5MT 4-6-0 No 45053 has just been given a good going-over by two young cleaners at the depot. This shows that, even in the twilight years of steam, a pride would still be taken at some depots to turn out clean locomotives. The shed code (64C) shows the locomotive is at its home depot; compare this photograph with that on page 85 showing the same locomotive at St Margarets depot in May 1966 in a desperately run-down condition.

Friday 16 July 1965
Ex-LMS Class 5MT 4-6-0 No 45477 simmers at the entrance to the shed, the locomotive's shedplate and buffer-beam inscription confirming that Dalry Road is its home depot. In September 1965 it had the distinction of hauling the last passenger train to leave Edinburgh Princes Street. Within three months of this photograph the depot would be closed and most of the locomotives reallocated to St Margarets or sent for scrap.

Around Edinburgh

IN those last few years before steam disappeared, the railway scene around Edinburgh was very mixed. While most of the named passenger express and inter-city trains were hauled by diesel locomotives or operated by diesel multiple-units, much of the rest remained steam-hauled. Goods trains, in particular, benefited from the availability of more powerful locomotives, and enthusiasts could regularly see the whole range of LNER Pacifics working on heavy goods trains over the Waverley Route between Edinburgh and Carlisle.

Putting aside the two main stations and the three locomotive depots (covered separately), there were still many sites around the city and the surrounding area where enthusiasts could watch steam locomotives performing on all types of duties. Edinburgh's suburban railway (Inner and Outer Circles), known locally as the 'Sub', had been 'dieselised' in 1960 and closed to passengers in September 1962, but it was still used by the bulk of goods traffic avoiding the city centre. The only station to maintain a semblance of a working goods yard was Duddingston & Craigmillar, which served the handful of operating breweries clustered round the railway. One in particular, Robert Deuchar, sent large amounts of draught beer in hogsheads to the Newcastle area virtually every day. Incoming traffic was mostly barley for the maltings or barley malt for the breweries, together with coal for the brewery boilers and, of course, the returning empty barrels. But, as the breweries closed during the early 1960s and traffic dwindled, the yard was used more often to store passenger carriages. A branch line from the yard served St Leonard's coal depot in the city, and regular trains of coal wagons were to be seen slogging up the 1-in-30 gradient to the yard — usually behind an ex-NBR Class J37 0-6-0.

Other sites around the city included Craigentinny carriage sidings, located on the down side of the East Coast main line, just to the west of Portobello station. All coaching stock for the express passenger traffic on the East Coast main line out of Waverley station was serviced here, and there was thus a constant stream of empty coaching stock. In the early 1960s the bulk of these trains would be hauled by a Class B1 4-6-0, banked by one of the many Class V1 or

V3 2-6-2 tanks allocated to St Margarets depot, but by the mid-1960s the 'V1s' and 'V3s' had gone and Standard Class 4MT 2-6-4 tanks had taken their place. On occasion the train locomotive would haul its own coaching stock to Waverley, producing the fine sight of a Pacific lifting a heavy train of empty stock out of the yard.

In the early 1960s the Lothians coalfield was still operating, there being many busy collieries around Edinburgh and its environs. The coalfield stretched from Newtongrange, south of Edinburgh, in a northeasterly direction under the Niddrie area towards Prestongrange colliery, on the shores of the River Forth. There were large modern collieries at Bilstonglen and Monktonhall, but the most southerly (and one of the oldest) was the Lady Victoria at Newtongrange, with its large sidings either side of the Waverley Route; there were always a handful of National Coal Board locomotives working around the pit-head and yards here. Niddrie, on the southeastern side of the city, was where the enthusiast could find the web of National Coal Board lines serving Niddrie and Woolmet collieries, along with the brickworks at Niddrie. These were connected to the British Railways system at Niddrie West Yard, and the small NCB shed there stabled about six locomotives, mostly Andrew Barclay 0-6-0STs, of which two or three would normally be in steam. The truncated remains of the system servicing the brickworks survived (using steam power) until the end of 1972.

The saddest sights during this period were to be seen at such places as Bathgate depot and Bo'ness dock. The former was still a working motive-power depot (64F), from where a small number of ex-NBR 0-6-0 locomotives serviced the local goods-only branches, but the shed was also used to store large numbers of locomotives that were surplus to requirements and waiting to go for scrap. Lined up there were ex-NBR tank and tender locomotives along with more modern examples such as ex-LNER Class V1 and V3 2-6-2Ts and Class V2 2-6-2s. For a short period in the early 1960s, Bo'ness dock sidings were used to store row upon row of ex-CR and ex-NBR tank and tender locomotives. For those enthusiasts who visited this cold and windswept spot, the sight that greeted them was grim

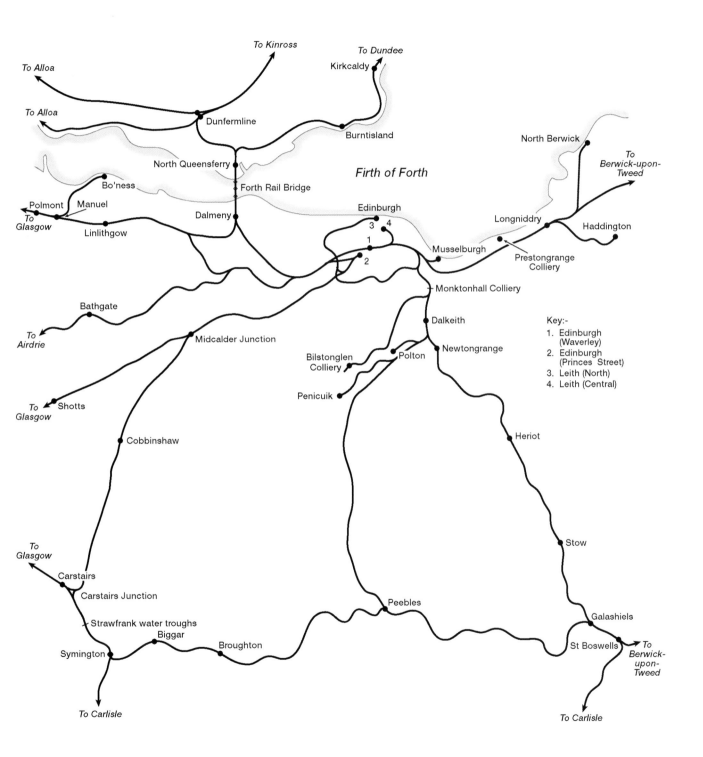

To Kinross

To Dundee

Kirkcaldy

To Alloa

To Alloa

Dunfermline

Burntisland

North Berwick

Firth of Forth

To Berwick-upon-Tweed

North Queensferry

Forth Rail Bridge

Bo'ness

Polmont   Manuel

Dalmeny

Edinburgh

3   4

Longniddry

Haddington

To Glasgow

Linlithgow

1

Musselburgh

Prestongrange Colliery

2

Bathgate

Midcalder Junction

Monktonhall Colliery

To Airdrie

Dalkeith

Key:-
1. Edinburgh (Waverley)
2. Edinburgh (Princes Street)
3. Leith (North)
4. Leith (Central)

Bilstonglen Colliery

Polton

Newtongrange

To Glasgow

Shotts

Penicuik

Cobbinshaw

Heriot

Stow

To Glasgow

Carstairs

Carstairs Junction

Peebles

Galashiels

Strawfrank water troughs

Biggar

Broughton

St Boswells

To Berwick-upon-Tweed

Symington

To Carlisle

To Carlisle

indeed, with these rows of rusting locomotives waiting to be towed away to the scrap merchants. Today, the site at Bo'ness is occupied by the SRPS and the Bo'ness & Kinneil Railway, which is home to three of the 10 pre-Grouping Scottish locomotives to survive in preservation. I have no doubt that the ghosts of those rows of condemned locomotives keep a guardian's eye over the site today.

In the 1960s short trips by rail could be made very easily from Edinburgh, and places such as Galashiels, Polmont and Midcalder Junction could be reached relatively quickly. At Galashiels station, on the Waverley Route, the enthusiast could witness the procession of goods trains working between Millerhill yard in Edinburgh and Kingmoor yard in Carlisle. A variety of LNER designs could be seen on this traffic —'V2' 2-6-2s, 'B1' 4-6-0s and, of course, the Pacific classes, particularly the 'A1s' and 'A3s'. Polmont depot (65K) was much quieter. This grimy shed was squeezed between the Edinburgh–Glasgow main line and the Union Canal, which was on a high banking on the south side of the shed; consequently the depot saw little direct sunlight. It stabled mostly ex-NBR 0-6-0 locomotives used on local goods trains to Bo'ness, Grangemouth and Edinburgh. A much brighter prospect was to travel to Midcalder and walk the last couple of miles or so from the station to the junction signalbox. There an enthusiast could watch the procession of passenger and goods workings that would pass throughout the day — all steam, with not a diesel in sight! These would include all passenger trains heading to/from Edinburgh Princes Street station and goods traffic to/from Slateford yard in Edinburgh. There was also much local coal traffic from the collieries in the Shotts area. Locomotives would, of course, be mainly LMS designs, but there were also some Standard types.

The early 1960s saw many railtours organised to visit the goods-only branch lines around Edinburgh that were facing closure. Some of these were memorable, towns visited being as diverse as Penicuik, in the deep valley of the River Esk, with its paper mills, and Haddington, with its distillery and wide farming vistas.

Any rail journey heading north from Edinburgh would pass over the immense, beautifully balanced structure of the Forth Bridge. Designed by Benjamin Baker and Sir John Fowler, it was opened officially on 4 March 1890 and reduced the journey times to Aberdeen, so much so, that a second round of the Railway Races to the North, first seen in 1888, took place in 1895, with trains competing on several nights over the East and West Coast routes to travel from London to Aberdeen in the shortest possible time. The enthusiast of the early 1960s could view the bridge from several directions — from the train passing over it (hopefully behind a steam locomotive), accompanied by the loud, distinctive rumbling of all that vibrating steel, or from either of the two stations at each end (Dalmeny on the southern side and North Queensferry opposite). Alternatively, and more unusually, the ferry trip across the River Forth at South Queensferry was worth the few shillings it cost to get a very different view of the bridge. This opportunity was lost to the traveller in September 1964, when the Forth Road Bridge was opened and the ferry crossing ceased.

Saturday 25 August 1962
In the goods yard at Duddingston & Craigmillar station, ex-NBR Class J35 0-6-0 No 64510 awaits arrival of the SLS 'Edinburgh and Dalkeith' railtour.

Saturday 25 August 1962
The SLS 'Edinburgh and Dalkeith' railtour has arrived at Duddingston & Craigmillar station behind ex-LNER Class V3 2-6-2T No 67668,. ex-NBR Class J35 0-6-0 No 64510 (also shown on previous page) has taken over to propel the train up the 1-in-30 gradient to St Leonards goods yard.

Saturday 25 August 1962
Having waited in Duddingston & Craigmillar station yard for the returning train, No 67668 departs with the next leg of the tour.

Above:
Saturday 3 February 1962
On this bright winter's day, ex-CR Class 3F 0-6-0 No 57550 works a local branch-line special from Edinburgh Princes Street. Seen at Murrayfield station, the locomotive would later run round at Leith North before heading off to other branch lines around Edinburgh.

Top right:
Saturday 25 August 1962
Duddingston & Craigmillar station stood next to several breweries that were still operating in the 1960s. Some of these buildings can be seen in the background as ex-LMS Class 6P5F 'Jubilee' 4-6-0 No 45588 *Kashmir* heads west with a goods train.

Lower right:
Saturday 4 May 1963
Bathgate depot still supplied some locomotives for the freight work in the area, but a large number of locomotives were also stored here awaiting their fate. One of these was ex-NBR Class J36 0-6-0 No 65267.

Saturday 23 March 1963
Standard Class 4MT 2-6-4T No 80006
nears the end of its journey from
Berwick-upon-Tweed to Edinburgh
Waverley at the head of a three-coach
stopping train. The driver appears
to be relaxing as he approaches
Portobello station, the last stop
before Waverley.

Saturday 3 November 1962
Class A1 4-6-2 No 60127 *Wilson
Worsdell*, bearing a Tweedmouth
(52D) shedcode, leaves Craigentinny
carriage sidings for Waverley with
empty coaching stock.

Saturday 15 June 1963
Crossing the immense and imposing
structure of the Forth Bridge,
Standard Class 6P5F 'Clan' No 72005
Clan Macgregor heads a passenger
train from Edinburgh Waverley to
Dundee and Aberdeen.

Saturday 6 July 1963
In comparison to the Class J36, the more powerful Class J37, introduced in 1924, certainly gave an air of strength. No 64537 is seen at Polmont depot, with another of the class, No 64551, in the background.

Saturday 15 February 1964
In charge of ex-LNER Class V2 2-6-2 No 60816, Driver W. Bell and an unidentified fireman from St Margarets depot wait for the 'off' at Longniddry station with a three-coach stopping train from Edinburgh to Berwick-upon-Tweed.

Sunday 2 February 1964
At the head of a rugby supporters' special returning from Cardiff, Class A1 4-6-2 No 60152 *Holyrood* makes a very slippery start from Galashiels station. The trackbed is now a roadway by-passing the centre of Galashiels.

Tuesday 16 July 1963
The crew of Andrew Barclay 0-6-0ST No 23 of the National Coal Board prepare to shunt some coal wagons at Niddrie brickworks.

Thursday 16 April 1964
Standing by the locomotive shed at Niddrie, another Barclay-built 0-6-0ST, No 19 of the Lothians Northern Area of the National Coal Board, has an extremely bent running plate as witness to some very heavy shunting.

Above:
Monday 17 May 1965
Ex-LNER Class A3 4-6-2 No 60041 *Salmon Trout* approaches Galashiels working an express goods from Carlisle to Edinburgh. Compare this photograph with that on page 93 of the same locomotive a year later.

Top right:
Saturday 13 June 1964
The rain has just stopped, and the crew of Standard Class 4 2-6-0 No 76050 attend to filling the tender with water at St Boswells station prior to departing with a train for the Tweed Valley line. This traversed the rolling agricultural countryside to Roxburgh, Kelso, Coldstream and Berwick-upon-Tweed. The section of line from St Boswells to Kelso was opened in June 1850 by the North British Railway. This day was the last of passenger operation on the line.

Lower right:
Saturday 7 November 1964
Standard Class 7P6F 'Britannia' 4-6-2 No 70013 *Oliver Cromwell* passes Midcalder Junction with a goods train from Edinburgh to the South. Built at Crewe Works in 1951, this locomotive became the last working survivor of the class, serving until the last days of steam in August 1968. It was subsequently preserved and can now be seen at the Bressingham Steam Museum in Norfolk.

Glasgow

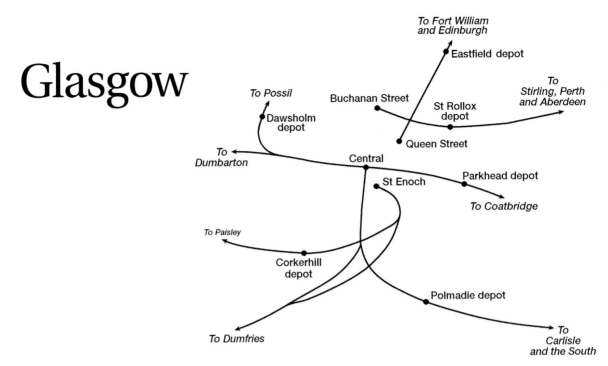

To Fort William
and Edinburgh

Eastfield depot

To Possil

Dawsholm
depot

Buchanan Street

St Rollox
depot

To
Stirling, Perth
and Aberdeen

Queen Street

To
Dumbarton

Central

St Enoch

Parkhead depot

To Coatbridge

To Paisley

Corkerhill
depot

Polmadie depot

To Dumfries

To
Carlisle
and the South

AS an Edinburgh enthusiast, I looked forward to visiting the Glasgow depots to observe the variety of classes that could be found there. They included Eastfield (65A), St Rollox (65B), Parkhead (65C), Dawsholm (65D), Kipps (65E), Polmadie (66A) and Corkerhill (67A). The latter could still be reached from central Glasgow by a tram service!

The larger depots — Polmadie, Eastfield, St Rollox and Corkerhill — were always bustling with activity, whilst the smaller ones seemed almost unused, with an air of desolation about them. These smaller depots — Parkhead, Dawsholm and Kipps — were storing more locomotives out of use than there were in service. This, of course, reflected the increasing use of diesel locomotives and the rate of line closures in the Glasgow area.

In the early 1960s there was still lots of steam to see on those visits to Glasgow, Polmadie shed usually being the first port of call. There would be ex-LMS 'Jubilee', 'Royal Scot', 'Coronation' and 'Black Five' locomotives visiting from more southerly depots, along with 'Britannias', 'Clans', and Standard Class 5MT 4-6-0s and Class 4MT 2-6-4 tanks. There might also be a sprinkling of Class A2 Pacifics.

At Eastfield, diesels were starting to outnumber steam locomotives, but I do recall noting ex-LNER Class V1 and V3 2-6-2 tanks, together with Class B1 4-6-0s and a few remaining ex-NBR 0-6-0 tank and tender classes.

At St Rollox depot, an enthusiast could always see some 'fresh from works' locomotives that were undertaking running-in duties. Most of the classes to be seen here were ex-LMS and Standard types; St Rollox had an allocation of Caprotti-fitted Standard Class 5MT 4-6-0s. There would also be one or two ex-LNER locomotives on shed, especially 'A4s' used on the fast Glasgow (Buchanan Street)– Aberdeen service. Other visitors included ex-LMS Class 5 'Crab' 2-6-0s and the occasional Class 8F Austerity 2-8-0 from Grangemouth.

Corkerhill depot, serving the ex-GSWR lines from St Enoch station, may not have been as large as Polmadie, but there must have been a certain proud streak in the shed staff, as the locomotives allocated there were always turned out well. Along with its large allocation of Standard Class 4MT 2-6-4 tanks, the depot had a few ex-LMS Class 5 'Crab' 2-6-0s and a number of Standard and ex-LMS Class 5MT 4-6-0s.

The smaller depots around Glasgow were always the places to see those 'last few of class' locomotives which were on the point of extinction prior to going to the scrap dealers — such classes as ex-NBR 'Y9' 0-4-0STs and 'J83' and 'J88' 0-6-0Ts, along with ex-CR '2P' 0-4-4Ts and '2F' and '3F' 0-6-0s. There being no Scottish equivalent of Woodham's of Barry, all would end up being scrapped at dealers around Scotland. One bright spot when visiting Dawsholm in the early 1960s was to see two of the locomotives then preserved on the Scottish Region — ex-CR 4-2-2 No 123 and ex-HR 'Jones Goods' 4-6-0 No 103. Also there, having been transferred from Boat of Garten, was ex-HR 'Small Ben' 4-4-0 No 54398 *Ben Alder*, awaiting a decision as to its fate; unfortunately this turned out to be the cutter's torch.

Friday 27 March 1964
Locomotives at Corkerhill depot always appeared to be turned out for duty looking cleaner than those from any other depot in Glasgow. Some would say the old 'Sou'west' pride was still shining through. Here Standard Class 4MT 2-6-4T No 80047 is looking particularly clean.

Friday 27 March 1964
At the head of a stopping train to Carlisle, Standard Class 7P6F 'Britannia' 4-6-2 No 70006 *Robert Burns* pauses at Motherwell station on its journey south.

Friday 27 March 1964
Sitting over one of the ashpits at Polmadie depot, ex-LMS Class 7P 'Royal Scot' 4-6-0 No 46166 *London Rifle Brigade* simmers quietly whilst disposal takes place.

Friday 27 March 1964
Awaiting its next duty at Polmadie depot is Class A2 4-6-2 No 60535 *Hornet's Beauty*, one of the A. H. Peppercorn developments, introduced in 1947, of Thompson's 'A2/3' design. In the background is Standard Class 5MT 4-6-0 No 73062.

Above:
Sunday 22 April 1962
At Motherwell depot, ex-LMS Class 3F 'Jinty' 0-6-0T No 47536 sits at the head of a line of dead locomotives including an ex-LMS 'Black Five.

Top right:
Sunday 22 April 1962.
At Hamilton depot, another line of dead locomotives, this time headed by veteran Class J72 0-6-0T No 68733, designed by Worsdell for the North Eastern Railway and introduced in 1898. The photograph shows a second, unidentified member of the class in the background, parked behind an unidentified ex-LMS Class 4MT 2-6-4T.

Lower right:
Saturday 30 March 1963.
Stored out of use at Polmadie depot at this time were five of the 10 Standard Class 6P5F 'Clan' 4-6-2 locomotives. Here we see No 72001 *Clan Cameron* between two of its classmates.

Saturday 30 March 1963
Class J83 0-6-0 tank No 68442, minus its coupling rods at Kipps depot. The 'J83' was another Holmes design, introduced in 1900.

Saturday 30 March 1963
At St Rollox depot a work-stained veteran, ex-NBR Class J36 0-6-0 No 65287, waits quietly for its next duty. This example has a cut-down cab, dome and chimney; compare this with the original, graceful design of its classmates on pages 97 and 105.

Saturday 30 March 1963
Several examples of veteran North British designs were stored at Kipps depot, awaiting their fate. Class Y9 0-4-0ST No 68104 is of Holmes design introduced in 1882.

Saturday 30 March 1963
Introduced in 1904 to a Reid design for the North British Railway, the Class J88 0-6-0T featured a very short wheelbase. The stovepipe chimney of No 68345 makes the locomotive look ugly; classmate No 68350, with original chimney, shows off its more graceful lines. Both are seen at Kipps depot.

Sunday 22 April 1962
Ex-LMS Class 2F 0-6-0T No 47168 is seen at Hamilton depot. Designed by Fowler for the LMS and introduced in 1928, this class of locomotive had a short wheelbase to facilitate dock working.

Friday 27 March 1964
Visiting from Ayr depot (67C),
ex-LMS Class 5 'Crab' 2-6-0 No 42737
was in good clean condition when
seen at Corkerhill depot.

Friday 27 March 1964
Seen reversing out of Glasgow
Central station towards Polmadie
depot, ex-LMS Class 8P 'Coronation'
4-6-2 No 46237 *City of Bristol* had
arrived earlier with a passenger
train from London.

Saturday 11 April 1964
Ex-LMS Class 7P 'Royal Scot' 4-6-0
No 46162 *Queen's Westminster
Rifleman* waits to leave Polmadie
depot for its next turn of duty.

Saturday 11 April 1964
At the head of a football special
returning to Edinburgh Princes Street,
Class 5MT 4-6-0 No 44702 prepares
to leave Kings Park station in
Glasgow.

The South West

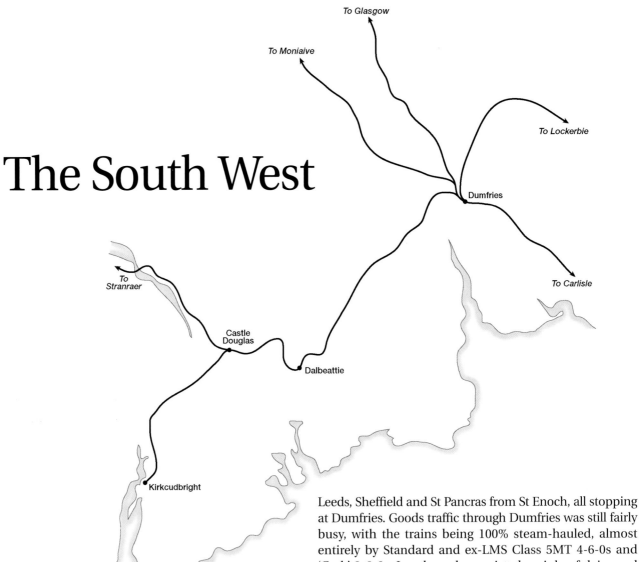

DURING 1964 I had the opportunity to make a couple of short visits to Dumfries and Kirkcudbright in southwest Scotland. Dumfries was an important railway junction, as all the passenger trains on the ex-GSWR line to Glasgow St Enoch and the 'Port Road' to Stranraer stopped there. The latter line, so named after the Portpatrick & Wigtonshire Railway, still boasted one named train every weekday. This was the overnight 'Northern Irishman' from London (Euston), which included some sleeper carriages and took almost 10 hours to reach Stranraer Harbour to connect with the morning ferry to Larne.

The other main line from Glasgow St Enoch still saw the 'Thames–Clyde Express' to London (St Pancras). This was usually hauled by an ex-LMS 'Royal Scot' or sometimes a 'Jubilee'. Additionally there were nine other daily services to Leeds, Sheffield and St Pancras from St Enoch, all stopping at Dumfries. Goods traffic through Dumfries was still fairly busy, with the trains being 100% steam-hauled, almost entirely by Standard and ex-LMS Class 5MT 4-6-0s and 'Crab' 2-6-0s. Local goods consisted mainly of dairy and agricultural produce heading for the markets in Glasgow or the South.

The small locomotive depot at Dumfries supplied Standard Class 4MT 2-6-4 tanks for the passenger service on the Kirkcudbright branch. For the Winter 1964 timetable, the branch from the junction at Castle Douglas had a service of four trains each way on weekdays, with no Sunday service. Kirkcudbright was a pretty holiday village with a busy harbour of fishing boats catching mainly scallops. In the summer it would be bustling with holidaymakers, and, on the days I travelled, the service was busy with passengers travelling to/from Dumfries. One service was even carrying some homing-pigeon baskets. There were still some goods workings on the branch, with dairy products coming from the local creameries. The branch closed to passenger traffic in May 1965.

Tuesday 28 January 1964
At Dumfries station on a cold winter's
night, ex-LMS Class 5MT 4-6-0
No 45126 waits at the head of a
passenger train from Carlisle.
The locomotive is in filthy condition,
its cabside number barely visible.
The AWS instrument can clearly be
seen in the cab.

Above:
Tuesday 28 January 1964
With a full head of steam, ex-LMS Class 5MT 4-6-0 No 45478 accelerates past Dumfries MPD at the head of a passenger train.

Below:
Tuesday 28 January 1964
In store at Dumfries, ex-CR '3F' 0-6-0 No 57600 awaits its fate.

Right:
Tuesday 28 January 1964
One of a number of ex-LMS Class 2P 4-4-0s allocated to southwest Scotland, No 40670 had been allocated to Ayr depot but was by now in store at Dumfries depot.

Top left:
Saturday 16 May 1964
In charge of an express goods from Carlisle, ex-LMS Class 5MT 4-6-0 No 44986 pauses in Dumfries station before leaving for Stranraer. The locomotive was allocated to Carlisle Kingmoor (12A) depot.

Lower left:
Saturday 16 May 1964
Ex-LMS Class 5 'Crab' 2-6-0 No 42739 simmers quietly at Dumfries depot. This class of powerful yet awkward-looking locomotives was designed by Hughes and first introduced in 1926. This example bears a Hurlford (67B) shed code.

Above:
Saturday 16 May 1964
Accelerating past the signalbox at Castle Douglas, the driver of Standard Class 4MT 2-6-4 tank No 80076 takes the tablet for the single-line branch to Kirkcudbright.

Saturday 16 May 1964
Standard Class 4MT 2-6-4T No 80076 has just arrived at Kirkcudbright from Dumfries with a well-patronised passenger train. The group of gentlemen on the platform are waiting for racing-pigeon baskets to be unloaded.

Saturday 16 May 1964
Having uncoupled from its train, Standard Class 4MT 2-6-4T No 80076 runs round before coupling up and heading the return service to Dumfries.

Strawfrank Troughs

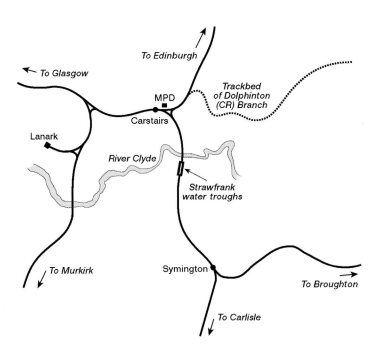

STRAWFRANK water troughs lay a mile or so south of Carstairs on the West Coast main line and were constructed by the LMS c1927 to facilitate the proposed non-stop running of express passenger trains to Glasgow and Edinburgh from the South by eliminating the need for water stops. This was a wonderful site for photographing or simply watching the traffic on the first and last Saturdays of the traditional Glasgow Fair holiday fortnight, which always fell in the latter half of July.

I managed to visit Strawfrank troughs on several Saturdays during July 1963 and again in July 1964. On these days what seemed a constant stream of both regular and special trains ran, virtually 100% steam-hauled, between Glasgow and the main holiday resorts in England (the Lancashire coast being favourite) and North Wales. The troughs could be approached by a walk down a minor road from Carstairs and lay immediately south of the rail bridge crossing the River Clyde. On a good, sunny day there were wonderful views of the river valley and the approaching trains leaving Carstairs. The troughs were used regularly on such days, mostly by traffic bound for Glasgow or Perth and the North but also on occasion by southbound trains. I am sure that, on those very busy Saturdays, goods trains were kept to a minimum so that as many operating paths as possible were allocated to special passenger workings. Diesel haulage could be seen on these days, but this was minimal and was restricted to named passenger expresses such as the 'Royal Scot' and 'Mid-day Scot'. Some double-heading of the heaviest passenger trains was required to assist on the long southbound climb to Beattock Summit, and pilot engines seen could vary from Fairburn 2-6-4 tanks to ex-LMS Class 5MT 4-6-0s and even English Electric Type 4 diesels.

I was fortunate, during these visits, to have witnessed possibly the last working Standard Class 6P5F 'Clan' light Pacifics. By this time, the five Scottish-allocated locomotives were stored out of use at Polmadie depot in Glasgow, but Carlisle Kingmoor's five were still occasionally to be seen working on the West Coast main line. All 10 were subsequently scrapped, but there are currently plans by the Standard Steam Locomotive Co to build a new 'Clan', No 72010 *Hengist*, which would be the 1,000th Standard locomotive to be built.

Carstairs, with its long, wide, sweeping island platform, was itself very busy with regular passenger workings. Local traffic from Lanark and Edinburgh crossed with trains from Glasgow and the North, and through coaches would be attached to the southbound passenger trains. Similarly, trains arriving from the South with through coaches for Edinburgh would stop in the down platform, where the coaches would be uncoupled, a locomotive hooked up and the train quickly despatched. For young enthusiasts, the station afforded the unique opportunity of waiting by the telegraph office for the progress board to be updated, and although this chalked-up information did not always prove accurate, it did give some indication of timings and as to what train was likely to be the next arrival from the South.

146

Saturday 27 July 1963

In store at Carstairs depot (66E), ex-CR Class 3P 4-4-0 No 54463 and classmate No 54502 await their fate. The class was designed by William Pickersgill, these two examples being built in 1916 and 1922 respectively. No 54463 became the last working member of the class and was withdrawn from traffic in December 1962 after helping to take the new Glasgow 'Blue Train' electric multiple-units to Hyndland depot for modifications to be carried out. These locomotives were fitted with Westinghouse air brakes, which were necessary for hauling the EMUs.

Saturday 13 July 1963
On a beautifully clear summer's day,
ex-LMS Class 5MT 4-6-0 No 45084,
allocated to Stirling depot (65J),
has its work cut out with a heavy
southbound train.

Saturday 13 July 1963
Ex-LMS Class 5MT 4-6-0 No 45484
working hard but still with a full
head of steam as it heads south
over the troughs.

Saturday 27 July 1963
The double-heading of heavily
loaded passenger trains was often
essential, and this 15-coach train
is a case in point. Robert Stephenson
& Hawthorn-built Type 4 No D318
pilots ex-LMS Class 5MT 4-6-0
No 45090 southbound over the
troughs. Built in 1961, No D318
(later numbered 40 118 and finally
97 408) lasted in service until 1985,
after which it passed into
preservation at the Birmingham
Railway Museum.

Saturday 27 July 1963
Class 5MT 4-6-0 No 44689 makes
a fine start heading south away
from Carstairs with a train of empty
coaching stock. This locomotive
was allocated to Carlisle Kingmoor
depot (12A).

Saturday 27 July 1963
A group of enthusiasts witness ex-LMS Class 7P 'Royal Scot' 4-6-0 No 46118 *Royal Welch Fusilier* with a six-coach stopping train from Glasgow to Carlisle.

Saturday 27 July 1963
Ex-LMS Class 6P5F 'Jubilee' 4-6-0 No 45742 *Connaught* takes water on board as it speeds northbound with a passenger train.
The locomotive's shedcode plate (12A) denotes allocation to Carlisle Kingmoor depot.

Saturday 27 July 1963
Ex-LMS Class 7P 'Royal Scot' 4-6-0
No 46155 *The Lancer* also takes water
as it passes over the troughs on a
northbound passenger train.

Saturday 18 July 1964
One of the few goods trains seen
on this day, ex-LMS Class 5MT 4-6-0
No 44953 of Carstairs depot (66E)
heads northbound on a through
goods train.

Left:
Saturday 18 July 1964
Another double-heading of a heavy passenger train; this time both locomotives are steam. Ex-LMS Class 5MT 4-6-0 No 45029 pilots Standard Class 6P5F 'Clan' 4-6-2 No 72007 *Clan Mackintosh* heading south over the troughs.

Above:
Saturday 18 July 1964
With a full head of steam, Standard Class 7P6F 'Britannia' 4-6-2 No 70038 *Robin Hood* picks up water as it heads north on an express passenger train.

Below:
Saturday 18 July 1964
Ploughing a lonely furrow, Standard Class 9F 2-10-0 No 92130 picks up water as it heads southbound, light-engine.

Saturday 18 July 1964
With an injector bursting into life,
Standard Class 7P6F 'Britannia' 4-6-2
No 70035 *Rudyard Kipling* heads
north over the troughs with a
passenger train. Originally allocated
to Norwich for fast services to/from
London (Liverpool Street), this
locomotive was transferred to the
London Midland Region in 1963
for services north of Crewe.

Saturday 18 July 1964
Yet another double-header
on a heavy passenger train.
English Electric Type 4 No D337
pilots Standard Class 6P5F 'Clan'
4-6-2 No 72008 *Clan Macleod*
on a southbound express.

Index of Photographic Locations